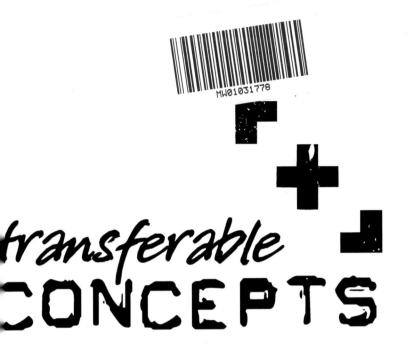

transferable
CONCEPTS

How *You* Can *Be Sure You Are* A *Christian*

BILL BRIGHT

How You Can Be Sure You Are a Christian

Cru
665 Hwy 74 South, Suite 350
Peachtree City, GA 30269

ISBN 978-1-56399-101-2

© 2009 Bright Media Foundation and Campus Crusade for Christ International (CCCI). © 1999 Bill Bright. "Bright Media Foundation" is a registered trademark of Bright Media Foundation, Inc. "Campus Crusade for Christ International" and "CCCI" are registered trademarks of Campus Crusade for Christ, Inc. All rights reserved. No part of this book may be reproduced, stored in a retrieval system, or transmitted in any form or by any means, except in the case of brief quotations printed in articles or reviews, without prior permission in writing from the publisher.

Design and typesetting by Tyrrell Creative and Regroup Design.

Printed in the United States of America.

Unless otherwise indicated, Scripture quotations are taken from the *New International Version*, © 1973, 1978, 1984 by the International Bible Society. Published by Zondervan Bible Publishers, Grand Rapids, Michigan.

Scripture quotations designated TLB are from *The Living Bible*, © 1971 by Tyndale House Publishers, Wheaton, Illinois.

WHAT IS A TRANSFERABLE CONCEPT?

hen our Lord commanded the eleven men with whom He had most shared His earthly ministry to go into all the world and make disciples of all nations, He told them to teach these new disciples all that He had taught them (Matthew 28:18–20).

Later the apostle Paul gave the same instructions to Timothy: "The things you have heard me say in the presence of many witnesses entrust to reliable men who will also be qualified to teach others" (2 Timothy 2:2).

In the process of counseling and interacting with tens of thousands of students, laymen, and pastors since 1951, our staff have discovered the following:

- Many church members (including people from churches that honor our Lord and faithfully teach His Word) are not sure of their salvation.
- The average Christian is living a defeated and frustrated life.
- The average Christian does not know how to share his faith effectively with others.

In our endeavor to help meet these three basic needs and to build Christian disciples, Campus Crusade for Christ has developed a series of "how to's"—or "transferable concepts"—in which we discuss many of the basic truths that Jesus and His disciples taught.

A "transferable concept" is an idea or a truth that can be transferred or communicated from one person to another and then to another, spiritual generation after generation, without distorting or diluting its original meaning.

As these basic truths—"transferable concepts"—of the Christian life are made available through the printed word, video and other multi-media in every major language of the world, they could well be used of God to help transform the lives of tens of millions throughout the world.

We encourage you to master each of these concepts by reading it thoughtfully at least six times[1] until you are personally prepared to communicate it to others "who will also be qualified to teach others." By mastering these basic materials and discipling others to do the same, many millions of men and women can be reached and discipled for Christ and thus make a dramatic contribution toward the fulfillment of the Great Commission in our generation.

Bill Bright

---

[1] Educational research confirms that the average person can master the content of a concept, such as this one, by reading it thoughtfully six times.

CONTENTS

How You Can Be Sure You Are a Christian

†

MILLIONS ARE NOT SURE

A prominent businessman, a leader in his church, sat across from me in my office. By every standard of human measure, this man was an outstanding success. As we talked, it became increasingly clear that in spite of his active leadership in the church, he was unsure of his eternal destiny. And he was desperately seeking assurance of his salvation.

The wife of an evangelist told me, "During the past thirty years, my husband and I have introduced thousands of people to Christ, but I have never been sure of my own salvation. Now, I'm desperate to know for sure. I need your help."

A student who had just received Christ stood to his feet. With a puzzled and troubled look on his face, he said, "I don't feel any different. I guess God didn't hear my prayer. How can I be sure Christ has come into my life?"

Perhaps you, too, are uncertain about your relationship with the Lord.

From my experience of counseling many thousands of students and laypeople throughout the years, I have become convinced that millions of church-goers have invited Christ into their lives, many of them over and over again, but are not sure of their salvation. In fact, surveys indicate that 50 percent of the church members in the United States are not sure Christ is in their lives. These are good people. Often, they have served faithfully in their church for years. And yet, they still have no assurance of Christ's abiding presence, no confidence that, if they died today, they would go to be with the Lord in heaven.

Why does this heartbreaking uncertainty exist among so many devoutly religious people? I am persuaded that their lack of assurance is due either to misinformation or to a lack of information regarding who God is. This includes understanding the deity of Christ, the meaning of the crucifixion and the resurrection of our Lord, and what is involved in receiving Jesus Christ as Savior and Lord.

Permit me to ask you this personal, so very important, question: What about you? If you were to die today, are you absolutely sure, beyond a shadow of a doubt, that you would go to heaven?

In the following pages, I want to share with you a message of great hope. It is a message for which the whole world hungers—and one I believe is desperately needed for the Church.

GREAT HUNGER FOR CHRIST

I have found a great and common hunger for Christ in men and women throughout the world. Let me give you just a few examples.

A friend asked me to meet with her brother. She was concerned for him because he was not a Christian. This man was one of the financial and political leaders of our country.

A meeting was arranged. After I introduced myself, we chatted briefly about the condition of the world and the need for a moral and spiritual awakening, all to which he agreed. I suggested to him that God had placed him in a unique position of leadership and he could have a real impact for helping to change the world for good. But first he would have to let God change him.

I shared with him a copy of the *Four Spiritual Laws* and asked him if he would like to read it with me. When we had finished reading the booklet, this famous and powerful man humbly said he would like to receive Christ. We prayed together. When we finished praying, he looked up and said to me, "I want you to know I really meant that. Tell me what I am supposed to do."

In Korea, approximately 10,000 students, laypeople, and pastors participating in a Campus Crusade for Christ training conference talked with more than 42,000 people during the training period about how to become a Christian. More than 16,000 people prayed with them to receive Christ. An additional 3,800 expressed a desire to be filled with the Holy Spirit.

In Haiti during a similar week of training, more than one thousand people received Christ in a single day when approximately five hundred pastors and lay leaders shared the gospel using the *Four Spiritual Laws* booklet. Vonette and I have visited the former Soviet Union many times in the past few years. What we have witnessed and heard is nothing less than miraculous. The spiritual hunger of the Soviet people and their openness to the gospel are far greater than we ever imagined. Christian leaders are spreading the gospel wherever they can with overwhelming response.

When Vonette spoke at a women's meeting—which was the first of its kind held on International Women's Day in the USSR—more than three hundred women packed out a century-old Protestant church to hear her speak. She shared from the Word for an hour, and her talk was followed by two-and-a-half hours of questions and answers, which further demonstrated the spiritual hunger there.

Tens of thousands of people in the former Soviet Union have received Christ as the result of viewing the *JESUS* film. Today, more than 425 million people worldwide have viewed the film with tens of millions expressing their desire to follow Christ as Savior and Lord.

Christians have found such openness to the gospel in Siberia that they have been showing the *JESUS* film around the clock, even in the dead of winter! It's an evangelistic schedule unheard of in the United States. Every two hours, *JESUS* is being shown in a packed room, even at midnight, 2 a.m., and 4 a.m. Starved for God for more than seventy years, the Soviet people willingly endure hardship, even the frigid Siberian nights, to learn about our wonderful Savior.

In Romania one man describes the openness for the gospel in his country. "Our people...are hungry. They are so hungry. Everyone we meet—young people, students—when we give them Christian books, they are so happy!" A Romanian pastor reports, "Every meeting we have five to six thousand people, and we have only 1,500 seats. The large majority stand three hours Sunday morning, two hours Sunday night, and two hours Friday night. The street and the corridor are packed with crowds. If it is raining or snowing or in the heat of the summer, they are there. It is something that warms my heart whenever I come to church and see crowds flowing from every street to that place. I just praise God!"

Missionaries in Western Europe who distribute Bibles to Eastern Europeans traveling through these countries also report great hunger for the Word of God. As these missionaries give out Christian literature on Bulgarian, Polish, Russian, Czechoslovakian, and Romanian ships, buses, and trains, they find hands eagerly reaching for the Bibles to satisfy deep spiritual needs.

Even the seamen on Cuban, Ethiopian, and Red Chinese vessels want to quench their spiritual thirst. One missionary reports that when he is allowed to board Chinese ships, he finds many sailors willing and anxious to accept free Bibles.

On one ship, his satchel full of Bibles and New Testaments was picked clean within seconds.

These examples are only a few of the many millions of people who are hungry for God throughout the world.

I believe billions of people are unsure of their relationship with God simply because they lack information. We must help them to understand that Christianity is not just a philosophy of life, not just a code of ethics, not just a standard of performance. Christianity is a personal relationship with the living, all-powerful Creator God through faith in His only begotten Son, our Lord Jesus Christ.

Take Buddha out of Buddhism, Mohammed out of Islam, and other religious founders out of their religions and little would be changed. But take Jesus Christ out of Christianity and nothing more than form and facade are left. Christianity is a personal relationship with the living Christ!

But how can you be sure of your relationship with Christ? I ask this all-important question again: If you were to die this very moment, do you know where you would spend eternity?

Perhaps you have only recently received Christ and are still not sure that anything has really happened—you are not confident of your salvation; you lack the assurance of your relationship with God.

I want to share with you several vital principles which can give you that assurance.

THREEFOLD COMMITMENT

Becoming a Christian involves receiving the Lord Jesus Christ—the gift of God's love and forgiveness—by faith (John 1:12; Ephesians 2:8,9). It results in a threefold commitment to a person, the Lord Jesus Christ. It is a commitment to Him of your intellect, emotions, and will. Let's examine, one by one, each of these elements of Christian commitment.

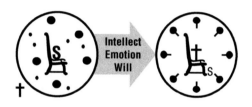

INTELLECTUAL COMMITMENT

Christianity is built on solid biblical and historical fact. To be sure you are a Christian, you must understand that Christianity is not a blind leap of faith. The truths of the Christian faith are documented by centuries of historical facts, study, and research. Many scholars have dedicated their lives to investigating the birth, life, teaching, miracles, death, resurrection, and influence of Jesus of Nazareth. As a result, we have overwhelming historical evidence proving all of the above.

The evidence includes writings of the contemporaries of Jesus whose lives were forever changed as a result of their intimate friendship with Him. Even Christ's enemies verified His resurrection through their conspiracy to pay witnesses to fabricate a story to explain why Jesus' tomb was empty.

Through these and many more convincing proofs, we know Jesus truly lived on earth; Jesus truly died; and Jesus truly rose again.

In the last years of his life, the German dramatist Johann Wolfgang von Goethe wrote, "If ever the Divine appeared on earth, it was in the person of Christ."[2] The Russian novelist and philosopher Fyodor Dostoevsky said, "Even those who have renounced Christianity and attack it, in their inmost being still follow the Christian ideal, for hitherto neither their subtlety nor the ardor of their hearts has been

---

[2] Johann Wolfgang von Goethe, *Conversations With Eckermann* (San Francisco: North Point Press, 1984), n.p.

able to create a higher ideal of man and of virtue than the ideal given by Christ of old. When it has been attempted, the result has been only grotesque."[3]

Dr. Charles Malik of Lebanon, former president of the United Nations General Assembly, said, "I really do not know what will remain of civilization and history if the accumulated influence of Christ, both direct and indirect, is eradicated from literature, art, practical dealings, moral standards, and creativeness in the different activities of mind and spirit." Napoleon Bonaparte, the famous French general, said during his exile, "I know men; and I tell you that Jesus Christ is no mere man. Between him and every other person in the world, there is no possible term of comparison. Alexander, Caesar, Charlemagne, and I have founded empires. But on what did we rest the creations of our genius? Upon force. Jesus Christ founded his empire upon love; and at this hour millions of men would die for him."[4]

Thomas Jefferson, third president of the United States and principal author of the Declaration of Independence, said, "Of all the systems of morality, ancient and modern, which have come under my observation, none appear to me so pure as that of Jesus."[5]

More important than what others say about Jesus Christ is what the Scripture says about Him.

Jesus Christ was God in flesh and blood. He came to earth to die in our place. He willingly took upon Himself the death each of us deserves. Through His death and resurrection, Jesus enables each one of us to receive eternal life and free access to almighty God.

---

[3] John Bartlett, *Familiar Quotations* (Boston: Little, Brown and Company, 1955), p. 618.

[4] Frank S. Mead, *The Encyclopedia of Religious Quotations* (Old Tappan, NJ: Fleming H. Revell Company, 1976), p. 88.

[5] Mead, *Religious Quotations*, p. 100.

Years ago a brilliant young student came to talk to me following one of my lectures at a major university. He was the head of the Communist movement on the campus. He accused me of trying to brainwash the students because I was more mature than they. And he resented me for presenting my Christian views to them, views that were obviously diametrically opposed to his Marxist beliefs.

Instead of arguing with him, I invited him to my home for dinner. We had a good conversation about many topics as we ate. After we had finished dessert, I reached for my Bible. "I would like to read something to you from the Bible," I said.

He reacted strongly. "I don't believe the Bible!" he declared. "I don't want to hear anything you read. I've read the Bible from cover to cover, and it's filled with contradictions and myths. I don't believe a word of it."

I responded by saying, "If you don't mind, I'll read a few portions anyway."

So I turned to the first chapter of the Gospel of John and read:

> *Before anything else existed, there was Christ, with God. He has always been alive and is himself God. He created everything there is—nothing exists that he didn't make. Eternal life is in him, and this life gives light to all mankind. His life is the light that shines through the darkness—and the darkness can never extinguish it.*
>
> *To all who received him, he gave the right to become children of God. All they needed to do was to trust him to save them. All those who believe this are reborn!—not a physical rebirth resulting from human passion or plan—but from the will of God.*
>
> *And Christ became a human being and lived here on earth among us and was full of loving forgiveness and truth. And some of us have seen his glory—the glory of the only Son of the heavenly Father!* (John 1:1–5,12–14, TLB).

"Let me read that," he said eagerly. "I don't remember reading it." He went over the passage thoughtfully and handed the Bible back to me without comment.

Then I turned to Colossians 1, beginning with verse 13, and read:

For he [God] has rescued us out of the darkness and gloom of Satan's kingdom and brought us into the Kingdom of his dear Son, who bought our freedom with his blood and forgave us all our sins.

Christ is the exact likeness of the unseen God. He existed before God made anything at all, and, in fact, Christ himself is the Creator who made everything in heaven and earth, the things we can see and the things we can't...; all were made by Christ for his own use and glory. He was before all else began and it is his power that holds everything together.

It was through what his Son did that God cleared a path for everything to come to him—all things in heaven and on earth—for Christ's death on the cross has made peace with God for all by his blood (Colossians 1:13–17, 20, TLB).

Again, he asked if he could read that passage for himself. Then I turned to Hebrews 1 and read verses 1 through 3.

Long ago God spoke in many different ways to our fathers through the prophets..., telling them little by little about his plans.

But now in these days he has spoken to us through his Son to whom he has given everything and through whom he made the world and everything there is.

God's Son shines out with God's glory, and all that God's Son is and does marks him as God. He regulates the universe by the mighty power of his command. He is the one who died to cleanse us and clear our record of all sin, and then sat down in highest honor beside the great God of heaven (TLB).

By this time, the young man was very sober. His whole attitude of belligerence and antagonism had changed. So I read 1 John 2:22,23:

Who is the greatest liar? The one who says that Jesus is not Christ. Such a person is antichrist, for he does not believe in God the Father and in his Son. For a person who doesn't believe in Christ, God's Son, can't have God the Father either. But he who has Christ, God's Son, has God the Father also (TLB).

When I finished reading, he was obviously moved. We chatted a bit. After a while he stood and prepared to leave. I asked if he would write in our guest book. He nodded.

After he wrote his name and address, he penned these words, "The night of decision."

Here was a young man who had come with fire in his eyes, full of resentment for anything Christian. However, through the simple reading of God's holy, inspired Word, the Holy Spirit brought this young man to the point of not only being able to intellectually accept what he heard, but to believe and receive it.

Following one of my talks about the uniqueness of Jesus, a brilliant Indian Hindu scholar with a double doctorate—one in physics and one in chemistry—came to me angry and impatient.

"I resent you Christians," he said. "I resent the arrogance with which you say you have the only way to God. I believe Christianity is one way, but only one way. Hinduism is another. Buddhism, Shintoism, and other religions are all ways to God."

As we talked and examined the Scripture together, he began to see that Christianity is uniquely different from other religions or philosophies. Christianity alone makes provision for man's basic need—the forgiveness of sin. He admitted that his diligent reading of the sacred Hindu writings and dutiful observance of the rites and rituals had never enabled him to find God personally. Finally, we got down on our knees together, and this young Hindu intellectual asked Jesus to forgive his sins and become his Savior.

To become a Christian you must squarely face the claims of Christ and believe intellectually that Jesus is God and died for your sins, was buried, and rose again. You must believe that He wants to come into your life to be your Savior and Lord.

EMOTIONAL COMMITMENT

Becoming a Christian also involves your emotions.

From the Scripture we know that God has emotions. He feels love, joy, sorrow, compassion, anger, disappointment, and many other emotions. The Bible also says that you are created in the image of God. As a part of His image, God has given you the capacity to experience emotions. Just about everything you do, from the time you awaken in the morning until you go to sleep at night, involves emotions.

Each person who receives Jesus Christ as his Savior and Lord will have a different kind of emotional experience. Paul met God through a dramatic encounter on the road to Damascus. Timothy, on the other hand, was raised in a Christian home where he came to know Christ at an early age and gradually grew in his faith.

One frequently hears Christians enthusiastically sharing how their dramatic encounters with Christ resulted in their being healed of drug addiction, gross immorality, or some other distressing problem. The fact that their lives were indeed changed validates their claims.

On the other hand, there are many who have knelt quietly in the privacy of their homes, as I did, or at a mountain retreat, or in a church sanctuary, and there received Christ into their lives with no dramatic emotional experience.

Emotions can be misleading. Probably no one issue has caused more people to lack the assurance of a vital relationship with God than a wrong emphasis on feelings. I have had moments of great joy, enthusiasm, and spiritual awareness. And I have also felt times of sorrow and disappointment. But I do not depend on these feelings to determine my union with God. My emotions can be very deceiving.

We are to live the Christian life by faith, not emotions. Yes, emotions have a place in your experience, but how you feel does not determine the truth of your life with Christ. Rather, your emotions are a result of your faith and obedience. Our Lord said, "The one who obeys me is the one who loves me; and because he loves me, my Father will love him; and I will too, and I will reveal myself to him" (John 14:21, TLB). The Book of Romans assures us, "In the gospel a righteousness from God is revealed, a righteousness that is by faith from first to last, just as it is written: 'The righteous will live by faith'" (Romans 1:17).

There is a place for emotions in the Christian experience, though you should not seek them nor attempt to recapture them from the past. While you should not ignore the value of legitimate emotions, it is more important to remember that you are to live by faith—in God and in His promises—and not by seeking an emotional experience.

An acquaintance brought his friend to see me, hoping that he might receive Christ, which he did. But during our conversation, it became apparent that my acquaintance, despite his concern for his friend, was himself not a Christian. So I asked him, "When did you become a Christian?"

"I'm not really sure that I am a Christian," he replied.

"Do you believe that Jesus Christ is the Son of God?"

"Yes."

"Do you believe that He died on the cross for your sins?"

"Yes."

"Do you believe that if you receive Jesus Christ as your Savior, He will come into your life and make you a child of God?"

"Yes."

"You would like to receive Him, wouldn't you?"

"Yes, I would. But I'm waiting for an experience. When my mother became a Christian, she had a dramatic emotional experience, and I've been waiting all these years for God to give me such an experience."

Although he was a professing Christian and active in his church, the thing that kept him from assurance of salvation was the wrong emphasis on emotions. I was able to explain to him that he did not have to look for an emotional experience, but could believe God's Word. Finally we bowed in prayer, and as a simple expression of faith, he received Jesus Christ as his Savior and Lord and rejoiced in the certainty that Christ was in his life.

VOLITIONAL COMMITMENT

Becoming a Christian not only involves your intellect and your emotions, it also involves your will. You must first be willing to obey God and His Word.

Christ emphasized the importance of man's will in relation to the assurance of salvation. Jesus said:

> *"If anyone chooses to do God's will, he will find out whether my teaching comes from God or whether I speak on my own. He who speaks on his own does so to gain honor for himself, but he who works for the honor of the one who sent him is a man of truth"* (John 7:17,18).

Some people are reluctant to obey Christ because they fear He will change their plans and take all the fun out of their lives.

One student with whom I counseled and prayed hesitated to receive Christ because he enjoyed his life of parties and sex. But through the prayers of fellow students and friends, this young man decided to obey Christ. He discovered that what he thought was an exciting life was nothing compared to the abundant life that the Lord Jesus gives. He became one of the most vital and fruitful Christians on campus.

This student had fought against God's will for his life until he realized the truth of Jesus' words:

"If any of you wants to be my follower, you must put aside your own pleasures and shoulder your cross, and follow me closely. If you insist on saving your life, you will lose it. Only those who throw away their lives for my sake and for the sake of the Good News will ever know what it means to really live.

"And how does a man benefit if he gains the whole world and loses his soul in the process? For is anything worth more than his soul? And anyone who is ashamed of me and my message in these days of unbelief and sin, I, the Messiah, will be ashamed of him when I return in the glory of my Father, with the holy angels" (Mark 8:34–38, TLB).

"Let me assure you that no one has ever given up anything—home, brothers, sisters, mother, father, children, or property—for love of me and to tell others the Good News, who won't be given back, a hundred times over, homes, brothers, sisters, mothers, children, and land— with persecutions!" (Mark 10:29,30, TLB).

A leading athletic coach held in high esteem by millions of people, a man of sterling character and tremendous ability, shared with me his reluctance to surrender his life fully to Christ. He feared that God would ask him to become a minister and to give up the joy and love of his life—teaching.

Many successful people have refused to follow Christ because they are afraid He will demand that they sell their possessions and give everything to the poor as Jesus told the rich young ruler to do (Mark 10:17–22). Although God does lead some people to give their possessions, He leads others to use their influence for Christ in other ways.

As you walk in faith and obedience to God as an act of your will and allow Him to change your life, you will gain increasing assurance of your relationship with Him. You will experience God's work in your life as He enables you to do what you could never have done on your own—things like being able to love someone who treats you badly, maintaining a spirit of peace while surrounded by great pressures and problems, developing a growing desire to reach other people with the love of Christ.

But, if you do not trust God and His plan for your life and obey His commands, you will inevitably have doubts about your salvation.

Some people refuse to receive Christ because of pride or self-will. For approximately fifty years, I have worked with the so-called intelligentsia. In all those years, I have not met one single person who has said, "I have considered all the historical evidence and the claims of Christ, and I cannot believe He is the Son of God."

Everyone I have counseled who has rejected Christ has always denied Him as a matter of the heart, not the head—a matter of the will, not the intellect. They have used intellectual issues as a smoke screen to cover the deeper issues of the heart.

Many years ago I met with a famous professor of a very prestigious seminary. He did not believe that Jesus is God, even though he had taught thousands of young students who became ministers. One day I was invited to visit this great scholar by a friend who was getting his doctorate under his supervision.

My friend explained, "He does not believe that the Bible is the Word of God, but he is a good man. I like him. He is personable and warm-hearted, and I think you might be able to communicate with him."

The professor's first words after our introduction were, "Mr. Bright, when you talk to students about becoming a Christian, what do you tell them?"

Knowing his reputation, I wanted to weigh my words carefully, but before I could reply, he asked a second question. "Better still, what would you tell me? I would like to become a Christian."

He went on to explain that he had recently been reading the Word of God with a new understanding. For a couple of years he had also been studying the writings of the church fathers and biographies of great heroes of the faith. As a result, he had become intellectually convinced that Jesus is the Son of God. But he did not know Him as his personal Savior.

I drew a circle on a piece of paper explaining, "This circle represents your life." In the circle I drew a throne and on the throne I wrote the letter "S" for self. I explained, "In order to become a Christian, you must receive Christ into your life as your Savior from sin and the Lord and Master of your life. You must surrender the control of your life to Him."

"That's my problem," he said. "Intellectual pride has kept me from doing this. I've received many honors in the academic world, and I haven't been willing to humble myself before God. For years I have denied the deity of Christ and have taught thousands of young men to do the same."

At that moment we were interrupted by a telephone call, and due to other scheduled appointments, we were unable to finish our conversation. He asked us to return two days later. When we returned, he took us into an office with no phones and, locking the door behind us, said, "I want you to know that I went this morning to one of the local churches, took communion, and prepared my heart for your coming. I have been meditating on the third chapter of John, and I

If you are living a Christ-directed life, you are yielding to Christ, and your interests are controlled by Him, resulting in harmony with God's plan for your life.

Our lives parallel that of a caterpillar crawling in the dust —an ugly, hairy worm. One day this worm weaves a cocoon about its body. From this cocoon emerges a beautiful butterfly. We do not understand fully what has taken place. We realize only that, where once a worm crawled in the dust, now a butterfly soars in the air.

So it is in the lives of Christians. Where once we lived on the lowest level as sinful, self-centered individuals, now as we trust and obey God, we dwell on the highest plane, experiencing full and abundant lives as children of God. This life begins by receiving Christ into your life as your Savior and Lord.

Some years ago, a woman who had just received Christ through the witness of a staff member asked me to talk to her father about Christ. He was the founder of one of the largest corporations in the world at that time. I visited him in his beautiful home. He was truly a great man. His bearing, his manner, everything about him suggested he was truly a statesman.

He showed me trophy room after trophy room filled with plaques and photographs of him with kings, presidents, and all kinds of celebrities. He was a great philanthropist who had given hundreds of millions of dollars to very worthwhile causes.

After awhile he said, "My daughter tells me you have something important to share with me."

With this invitation, I began to talk with him about his relationship with Christ. He was very gracious, very warm, very open and responsive. I shared with him the words of our Lord in His discussion with Nicodemus, a Jewish religious leader who was deeply religious, moral, ethical, and above reproach. I read from the Gospel of John, chapter 3:

Jesus declared, "I tell you the truth, no one can see the kingdom of God unless he is born again."

"How can a man be born when he is old?" Nicodemus asked. "Surely he cannot enter a second time into his mother's womb to be born!"

Jesus answered, "I tell you the truth, no one can enter the kingdom of God unless he is born of water and the Spirit. Flesh gives birth to flesh, but the Spirit gives birth to spirit. You should not be surprised at my saying, 'You must be born again'" (John 3:3–7).

At this point this dear, gracious man in his middle eighties said to me, "Mr. Bright, I've been the chairman of the board of my church for fifty years, and no one has ever told me that I have to receive Christ as my Savior or that I have to be born again! Do you think, in the light of all of the good things I have done through the years, that I must be born again?"

I explained, "The need for you to be born again is not my suggestion. It is Jesus who said, 'You must be born again' to Nicodemus, who was also a fine leader and very religious."

Then I asked him, "Would you like to be born again?"

"Yes, I would," he replied.

YOU CAN BE SURE

You may say, "I believe Jesus Christ is the Son of God and died for my sins. Am I not a Christian?" You are not, if you have refused to surrender your will to Him.

Or you may say, "I heard a wonderful sermon, my emotions were stirred, and I had a great emotional 'spiritual' experience. I even responded to the invitation to go forward for counsel. Am I not a Christian?" You are not, if you have never relinquished the throne of your life, your will, to Christ.

Trustworthy Word
Confirming Holy Spirit   **Assurance**
Changed Life

How, then, can you be sure that you are a Christian? Is there not some kind of confirmation that God gives to those who sincerely receive Christ? I believe there is a threefold confirmation that Jesus Christ is in our lives.

EXTERNAL WITNESS OF GOD'S WORD

The promise of God's Word, not your feelings, is your authority. His Word is totally reliable. As a Christian you are to live by faith in the trustworthiness of God and His holy, inspired Word.

For years Martin Luther, the father of the Reformation, had attempted to earn his salvation by his dedication and good works. When he discovered that great biblical truth, "The righteous will live by faith" (Romans 1:17), his life was dramatically changed, and he no longer labored for the assurance of his destiny in Christ. He believed what God's Word had to say and had assurance of his salvation.

John Wesley, founder of the Methodist Church, was not sure of his salvation as a young man even though he was the son of a minister, the leader of the Holy Club at Oxford, and a missionary to the Indians of America. Upon his return to England, he met Jesus Christ at an Aldersgate meeting where he heard the reading of Martin Luther's treatise on faith as a preface to the Book of Romans. Wesley explained what happened in his autobiography. "About a quarter before nine, while he was describing the change that God works in the heart through faith in Christ, I felt my heart strangely warmed. I felt I did trust in Christ, and Christ alone, for my salvation—and an assurance was given me that

He had taken away my sins, even mine, and saved me from the law of sin and death."

Before the experience at Aldersgate, Wesley had engaged in a frenzied effort to try to earn God's salvation by his good works. There he received the assurance of God's salvation by faith.

First John 5:11,12 confirms that Christ is in your life if you received Him:

This is the testimony: God has given us eternal life, and this life is in his Son. He who has the Son has life; he who does not have the Son of God does not have life.

John 1:12,13 echoes this promise:

To all who received him, to those who believed in his name, he gave the right to become children of God—children born not of natural descent, nor of human decision or a husband's will, but born of God.

A doctor and his wife from Zurich, Switzerland, sent their son to the University of California, Los Angeles, to complete his doctoral studies in meteorology. Their son Hans received Christ at one of our meetings and wrote to his parents about his newfound faith. He mentioned my name as the one who had introduced him to our Lord. They wrote back asking if he would set up an appointment for them to see me so they might also receive Christ. At great expense, the father, mother, and their daughter flew all the way from Zurich to Los Angeles for the express purpose of becoming Christians.

This was at the beginning of the ministry of Campus Crusade. I never had anyone even walk around the corner to see me, yet these people were coming all the way from Switzerland. It was a dramatic moment for me when this man of great influence and means, with his wife, came into my office near the UCLA campus.

He began our meeting explaining his own spiritual journey. "I was an atheist for years," he said, "but I found no future in atheism. So, I began to study the religions of the Orient. Again, there was no satisfaction. Then, someone told me the New Testament was where I would find my answers. I began to read it and became convinced that Jesus was the one I was looking for. Then we received the letter from Hans telling us how you had helped him to become a Christian. We want you to tell us what you told Hans."

Well, you can imagine how I felt. What a privilege it was to talk to this wonderful couple about our Savior, the living Christ.

I explained how they could receive Christ by simply inviting Him into their lives. He interrupted me. "Mr. Bright," he said, "I've already done that. I receive Jesus into my life every day. On some occasions I ask Him in several times a day."

Now I was puzzled. Relatively new in leading people to the Lord at that time, I didn't know what to say. I prayed silently, "God, help me. What do I say now?"

There flashed in my mind Ephesians 2:8,9:

It is by grace you have been saved, through faith—and this not from yourselves, it is the gift of God—not by works, so that no one can boast.

I explained that it is not enough to ask Jesus into your life; you must believe He will come in as He promised. Faith says, "I know Jesus Christ is the Son of God." Faith says, "I know Jesus died for my sins." Faith says, "I know if I open my heart's door to Him, He will come in." Faith says, "When He comes in, I'll become a child of God." Faith says, "I know that, when I receive Jesus into my life, I will have eternal life."

I told the couple, "God honors faith. He does not honor your invitation to Him to come in. It is your faith in Him and His promise that, if you open the door, He will come in (Revelation 3:20) that He honors. You can ask Jesus into your life a thousand times, and He will never come unless you believe, on the basis of His promise, that He will come. You can depend on Him to keep His promise to come in if you ask Him in as an expression of faith."

I suggested that they invite Christ into their lives one more time and that this time they believe His promises that, if they will open the door, He will come in and that "to all who received him, he [God] gave the right to become children of God" (John 1:12, TLB).

Even before we prayed, the father's face lit up with assurance of his salvation, and he began to laugh. He was filled with wonder, gratitude, relief, praise, and thanksgiving. At last he had found the One for whom he had sought for many years.

He turned to his dear wife and spoke to her in German, telling her what I had shared with him. She too began to laugh with what I discovered later was a laugh of assurance. They had been looking for God, and now the light went on, and they were filled with joy.

They met the Savior, and oh, how their lives were changed. Later that night I had the privilege of praying with their daughter, who also received Christ. The entire family—father, mother, brother, sister—was united in Christ. Eventually, I had the opportunity to visit them in Zurich and saw further the miracle of God's grace in their lives.

I was telling that story later to a gathering of people at one of our training conferences. A woman in her eighties came up to me afterward. Her hair was snow white and her radiant face was stained with tears.

She said, "I've been a Sunday school teacher for more than forty years. Every day of my life, I have asked Jesus into my life, and I've never been sure He was there. Tonight, by faith, I asked Him in for the last time as you told the story of the man from Switzerland. Now I know He's there because He said He would come in. He promised never to leave me nor forsake me. I'm never going to insult Him by asking Him in again. For the rest of my life, as an expression of faith, I'm going to begin every day thanking Jesus that He is with me as He promised."

INTERNAL WITNESS OF THE HOLY SPIRIT

The apostle Paul writes, "The Spirit himself testifies with our spirit that we are God's children" (Romans 8:16). Paul emphasized the validity of this inner source of assurance to the Thessalonian converts:

> *When we brought you the Good News, it was not just meaningless chatter to you; no, you listened with great interest. What we told you produced a powerful effect upon you, for the Holy Spirit gave you great and full assurance that what we said was true* (1 Thessalonians 1:5, TLB).

CHANGED LIFE

Your changed life is a witness to the fact that you are a Christian. Paul records, "When someone becomes a Christian he becomes a brand new person inside. He is not the same anymore. A new life has begun!" (2 Corinthians 5:17, TLB). John says:

> *How can we be sure that we belong to him? By looking within ourselves: are we really trying to do what he wants us to? Someone may say, 'I am a Christian; I am on my way to heaven; I belong to Christ.' But if he doesn't do what Christ tells him to, he is a liar. But those who do what Christ tells them to will learn to love God more and more. This is the way to know whether or not you are a Christian. Anyone who says he is a Christian should live as Christ did* (1 John 2:3–6, TLB).

I remember well the night I prayed, "God, what do You want me to do with my life?" It was a simple, quiet prayer. But I meant what I prayed, and God heard me.

My life began to gradually change as I studied the Scriptures with other believers in the First Presbyterian Church of Hollywood. With the passing of time, I began to feel the assurance of God's love and forgiveness. My relationship with Him became the most important experience in my life.

If you have never personally received Jesus Christ, or if you have any doubts about your salvation, you can receive Him right now through faith. You can open the door of your life to Christ by expressing your faith to Him in prayer. The following prayer may express your desire:

> *Lord Jesus, I need You. Thank You for dying on the cross for my sins. I open the door of my life and receive You as my Savior and Lord. Thank You for forgiving my sins and giving me eternal and abundant life. Take control of my life. Make me the kind of person You want me to be.*

You do not become a Christian by simply praying this or any other prayer. You become a Christian by faith and by faith alone. Faith is putting your trust in God and His promises. I encourage you to say this prayer aloud in faith, for it is through prayer—talking to God—that you can express your faith in Christ and the promises of His Word.

Jesus would not deceive you. You can be sure, if you asked Him into your life, that He now lives inside you and will give you the abundant, eternal life He promised.

I encourage you, right now, to thank God for His faithfulness to you and for His presence in your life. Do not depend on your feelings. God's Word is your authority. Faith and obedience always result in the awareness of our Lord's presence (John 14:21).

Begin to spend some time each day in Bible study and prayer. It is best to set aside a particular time each day to do this and to make it a habit. This will help you grow and mature in your faith.

Become associated with vital Christians. If you do not belong to a local church, don't wait to be invited. Take the initiative; call the pastor of a nearby church where Christ is honored and God's Word is preached. Make plans to start this week and to attend regularly. If you have not already been baptized, plan to be baptized as an outward expression of your identification with Christ.

Now that you are sure you are a Christian, I encourage you to experience the joy of helping others receive Christ. Share your faith in Christ with your friends and neighbors at every opportunity. The apostle Paul was so excited about Jesus that he exclaimed in Colossians 1:28, "Everywhere we go we talk about Christ to all who will listen" (TLB). Take the initiative to tell everyone you meet about the person and claims of our Lord Jesus Christ and the revolutionary way He can change their lives—and how they, too, can be sure they are a Christian.

NOTE

Remember, *How You Can Be Sure You Are a Christian* is a transferable concept. You can master it by reading it six times; then pass it on to others as our Lord commands us in Matthew 28:20, "Teach these new disciples to obey all the commands I have given you" (TLB). The apostle Paul encouraged us to do the same: "The things you have heard me say in the presence of many witnesses entrust to reliable men who will also be qualified to teach others" (2 Timothy 2:2).

SELF-STUDY GUIDE

1. Why do some Christians lack the assurance of their salvation? (See pages 7,8.)

2. What do you believe intellectually about Christ? By what evidence do you know these beliefs to be true? (See pages 12,13.)

3. According to the following passages, who is Jesus Christ?

   a. Mark 1:1

   b. John 1:1,14

   c. John 10:30

   d. John 14:6

4. Why were Jesus' miracles recorded for us? (See John 20:30,31.)

5. Why did Jesus have to die?

   a. Hebrews 9:22

   b. 1 Peter 1:18,19

   c. 1 Corinthians 15:3

6. In John 1:12, what is the relation between the words "receive" and "believe"?

7. What does knowing who Jesus Christ is mean to you?

8. Based on the following verses, what scriptural assurances do you have that your salvation is more than emotion?

   a. Romans 8:16

   b. Ephesians 1:3–11

   c. 1 John 5:11–13

9. What emphasis do you think Christ placed on emotions during His earthly ministry? What do these two Scripture passages show?

   a. Mark 8:12

   b. Luke 10:21

10. How can emotions deceive you? (See pages 17–19.)

11. What happens as you begin to know God better? (See page 21.)

12. What does God's Word say about faith? (See Romans 1:17; 14:23; Hebrews 11:6.)

13. Why does becoming a Christian involve an act of the will? And why are some people reluctant to accept Christ? (See 2 Corinthians 4:3,4.)

14. How can you give God control of your life? (See page 22.)

15. What kind of confirmation should you have that you have become a Christian? (See pages 28–34.)

16. From Mark 8:34–38; 10:21,29,30; and John 3:3,16–21, explain Christ's advice and promises to those who hesitate to accept Him as Savior.

17. How can you be sure of your salvation and position in Christ? (See John 3:16; 10:28,29; 1 John 5:11–13.)

18. How would you relate Matthew 21:22 to salvation and a Christian's assurance of his salvation?

19. Think of someone who is unsure of his salvation. What will you do this week to help this person gain assurance of his salvation and realize his position in Christ?

GROUP DISCUSSION QUESTIONS

1. Christianity is built on biblical and historical fact. Discuss what facts are most important in making a commitment to Christ.

2. Why is Christianity different from all other religions? What does this difference mean to you personally?

3. The Christian life is to be lived by faith, not emotions. What place does emotion have in your Christian life? How and when can emotions be misleading? Share with the group a time in your life when you especially had to apply this truth.

4. Some people are reluctant to become Christians because they fear God will change their plans. Discuss an area in your life in which you saw God do this. What were the results?

5. Why is it important that you be sure of your salvation?

6. Church history records no great personal or group revivals that have taken place apart from an emphasis on God's holy Word. How does this emphasis affect the corporate life and witness of the church today? What role does God's Word play in your assurance of salvation?

7. With whom would you most like to share Christ right now? Break into pairs, discuss a strategy for reaching that person, and pray with your partner for him/her.

FASTING & PRAYER

In 1994, I felt led by God to undergo a 40-day fast. During that time, God impressed on me that He was going to send a great spiritual awakening to America, and that this revival would be preceded by a time of spiritual preparation through repentance, with a special emphasis on fasting and prayer. In 2 Chronicles 7:14, God gives us a promise of hope that involves repentance:

If my people, who are called by my name, will humble themselves and pray and seek my face and turn from their wicked ways, then will I hear from heaven and will forgive their sin and will heal their land.

Fasting is the only spiritual discipline that meets all the conditions of 2 Chronicles 7:14. When a person fasts, he humbles himself; he has more time to pray; he has more time to seek God's face, and certainly he would turn from all known sin. One could read the Bible, pray, or witness for Christ without repenting of his sins. But one cannot enter into a genuine fast with a pure heart and pure motive and not meet the conditions of this passage.

Because of this promise, God has led me to pray that at least two million North Americans will fast and pray for forty days for an awakening in America and the fulfillment of the Great Commission. As millions of Christians rediscover the power of fasting as it relates to the holy life, prayer, and witnessing, they will come alive. Out of this great move of God's Spirit will come the revival for which we have all prayed so long, resulting in the fulfillment of the Great Commission.

I invite you to become one of the two million who will fast and pray for forty days. For more information on fasting & prayer visit our web site and check out our section on Revival, Fasting & Prayer.

OTHER RESOURCES BY BILL BRIGHT

RESOURCES FOR FASTING AND PRAYER

The Coming Revival: America's Call to Fast, Pray, and "Seek God's Face." This inspiring yet honest book explains how the power of fasting and prayer by millions of God's people can usher in a mighty spiritual revival and lift His judgment on America. *The Coming Revival* can equip Christians, their churches, and our nation for the greatest spiritual awakening since the first century.

7 Basic Steps to Successful Fasting and Prayer. This handy booklet gives practical steps to undertaking and completing a fast, suggests a plan for prayer, and offers an easy-to-follow daily nutritional schedule.

Preparing for the Coming Revival: How to Lead a Successful Fasting and Prayer Gathering. In this easy-to-use handbook, the author presents step-by-step instructions on how to plan and conduct a fasting and prayer gathering in your church or community. The book also contains creative ideas for teaching group prayer and can be used for a small group or large gatherings.

The Transforming Power of Fasting and Prayer. This follow-up book to *The Coming Revival* includes stirring accounts of Christians who have participated in the fasting and prayer movement that is erupting across the country.

RESOURCES FOR GROUP AND INDIVIDUAL STUDY

Five Steps of Christian Growth. This five-lesson Bible study will help group members be sure that they are a Christian, learn what it means to grow as a Christian, experience the joy of God's love and forgiveness, and discover how to be filled with the Holy Spirit. Leader's and Study Guides are available.

Five Steps to Sharing Your Faith. This Bible study is designed to help Christians develop a lifestyle of introducing others to Jesus Christ. With these step-by-step lessons, believers can learn how to share their faith with confidence through the power of the Holy Spirit. Leader's and Study Guides are available.

Five Steps to Knowing God's Will. This five-week Bible study includes detailed information on applying the Sound Mind Principle to discover God's will. Both new and more mature Christians will find clear instructions useful for every aspect of decision-making. Leader's and Study Guides are available.

Five Steps to Making Disciples. This effective Bible study can be used for one-on-one discipleship, leadership evangelism training in your church, or a neighborhood Bible study group. Participants will learn how to begin a Bible study to disciple new believers as well as more mature Christians. Leader's and Study Guides are available.

Ten Basic Steps Toward Christian Maturity. These time-tested Bible studies offer a simple way to understand the basics of the Christian faith and provide believers with a solid foundation for growth. The product of many years of extensive development, the studies have been used by thousands. Leader's and Study Guides are available.

Introduction: The Uniqueness of Jesus
Step 1: The Christian Adventure
Step 2: The Christian and the Abundant Life
Step 3: The Christian and the Holy Spirit
Step 4: The Christian and Prayer
Step 5: The Christian and the Bible
Step 6: The Christian and Obedience
Step 7: The Christian and Witnessing

Step 8: The Christian and Giving
Step 9: Exploring the Old Testament
Step 10: Exploring the New Testament

A Handbook for Christian Maturity. This book combines the *Ten Basic Steps* Study Guides in one handy volume. The lessons can be used for daily devotions or with groups of all sizes.

Ten Basic Steps Leader's Guide. This book contains teacher's helps for the entire *Ten Basic Steps* Bible Study series. The lessons include opening and closing prayers, objectives, discussion starters, and suggested answers to the questions.

RESOURCES FOR CHRISTIAN GROWTH

Transferable Concepts. This series of time-tested messages teaches the principles of abundant Christian life and ministry. These "back-to-the-basics" resources help Christians grow toward greater spiritual maturity and fulfillment and live victorious Christian lives. These messages, available in book format and on video, include:

How You Can Be Sure You Are a Christian
How You Can Experience God's Love and Forgiveness
How You Can Be Filled With the Spirit
How You Can Walk in the Spirit
How You Can Be a Fruitful Witness
How You Can Introduce Others to Christ
How You Can Help Fulfill the Great Commission
How You Can Love By Faith
How You Can Pray With Confidence
How You Can Experience the Adventure of Giving
How You Can Study the Bible Effectively

A Man Without Equal. This book explores the unique birth, life, teachings, death, and resurrection of Jesus Christ and shows how He continues to change the way we live and think today. Available in book and DVD formats.

Life Without Equal. This inspiring book shows how Christians can experience pardon, purpose, peace, and power for living the Christian life. The book also explains how to release Christ's resurrection power to help change the world.

Have You Made the Wonderful Discovery of the Spirit-Filled Life? This booklet shows how you can discover the reality of the Spirit-filled life and live in moment-by-moment dependence on God.

The Secret: How to Live with Purpose and Power. In this inspiring book, best-selling author Bill Bright shows you how to discover a new dimension of happiness and joy in your Christian walk.

His Intimate Presence: Experiencing the Transforming Power of the Holy Spirit. Dr. Bill Bright explores what the Holy Scriptures teaches about the amazing presence and power of God's Spirit.

RESOURCES FOR EVANGELISM

Witnessing Without Fear. This best-selling, Gold Medallion book offers simple hands-on, step-by-step coaching on how to share your faith with confidence. The chapters give specific answers to questions people most often encounter in witnessing and provide a proven method for sharing your faith.

Reaching Your World Through Witnessing Without Fear. This six-session DVD provides the resources needed to sensitively share the gospel effectively. Each session begins with a captivating dramatic vignette to help viewers apply the training. DVD package includes all print materials on CD-ROM.

Have You Heard of the Four Spiritual Laws? This booklet is one of the most effective evangelistic tools ever developed. It presents a clear explanation of the gospel of Jesus Christ, which helps you open a conversation easily and share your faith with confidence.

Would You Like to Know God Personally? Based on the *Four Spiritual Laws*, this booklet uses a friendly, conversational format to present four principles for establishing a personal relationship with God.

Jesus and the Intellectual. Drawing from the works of notable scholars who affirm their faith in Jesus Christ, this booklet shows that Christianity is based on irrefutable historic facts. Good for sharing with unbelievers and new Christians.

A Great Adventure. Written as from one friend to another, this booklet explains how to know God personally and experience peace, joy, meaning, and fulfillment in life.

RESOURCES BY VONETTE BRIGHT

The Joy of Hospitality: Fun Ideas for Evangelistic Entertaining. Co-written with Barbara Ball, this practical book tells how to share your faith through hosting barbecues, coffees, holiday parties, and other events in your home.

The Joy of Hospitality Cookbook. Filled with uplifting Scriptures and quotations, this cookbook contains hundreds of delicious recipes, hospitality tips, sample menus, and family traditions that are sure to make your entertaining a memorable and eternal success. Co-written with Barbara Ball.

Beginning Your Journey of Joy. This adaptation of the *Four Spiritual Laws* speaks in the language of today's women and offers a slightly feminine approach to sharing God's love with your neighbors, friends, and family members.

*These fine products from Cru are available from New Life Resources at **800-827-2788** or online at **www.crustore.org.***

BILL BRIGHT was the founder and president of Campus Crusade for Christ International, the world's largest Christian ministry which serves people in 191 countries through a staff of 26,000 full-time employees and more than 225,000 trained volunteers.

Dr. Bright did graduate studies at Princeton and Fuller Theological seminaries and was the recipient of five honorary doctorates as well as many national and international awards. In 1996 Bright was presented with the prestigious Templeton Prize for Progress in Religion, for his work with fasting and prayer. Worth more than $1 million, the Templeton Prize is the world's largest financial annual award. Bright donated all of his prize money to causes promoting the spiritual benefits of fasting and prayer.

In 2000, Bright received the first Lifetime Achievement Award from his alma mater, Northeastern State University. In that same year, Bright and his wife were given the Lifetime Inspiration Award from Religious Heritage of America Foundation. Additionally, he received the Lifetime Achievement Award from both the National Association of Evangelicals and the Evangelical Christian Publishers Association. In 2002, Dr. Bright was inducted into the National Religious Broadcasters Hall of Fame. He authored over 100 books and publications committed to helping fulfill the Great Commission.

Before Dr. Bright went home to be with the Lord on July 19, 2003, he established Bright Media Foundation to promote and extend his written legacy to future generations.

YOUR CHANCE TO RESPOND

Have you received Jesus Christ as your Savior and Lord as a result of reading this book?

Go here: **http://www.campuscrusade.com/receive.htm**

http://looktoJesus.com

Are you a new Christian and want to know Christ better and experience the abundant life in Christ?

Go here: **http://www.cruresources.com**

http://growinginChrist.com

Do you want free information on staff and ministry opportunities with Campus Crusade for Christ?

Go here: **http://www.cru.org**

Would you like free information about other books, booklets, audio and video resources by Bill and Vonette Bright?

Go here: **http://www.crustore.org**

Or, you can send us an email at
customerservice@crustore.org.

Or, you can write us:
Cru
665 Hwy 74 South, Suite 350
Peachtree City, GA 30269